GANDHI

BeN

London

- He was transformed into a more religious person

- He staid true to his mom

In 1888, an unknown law student from India sat down to eat in the Central, a London restaurant that specialized in vegetarian food. The nineteen-year-old Mohandas K. Gandhi was lonely and displaced in the cold, rainy city where he was studying for a law degree. He was a long way from his warm, sunny home in Porbandar, India, where extended family had meant he was never alone, never lonely, and never without someone nearby who was quick to offer an opinion or advice.

The sea voyage to London had taken a full eight weeks. Once there, he struggled with the English language, and his innate shyness made it difficult for him to connect with people. His life in London was made even more difficult by a vow Gandhi had made to his very devout mother, Putlibai, before leaving India. He had solemnly promised her not to imbibe alcohol, not to engage in extra-marital sex, and not to eat meat—in keeping with the strictures of Hinduism in which she had raised him.

But London—England, in general, it seemed—was a meat-eating culture. Committed to vegetarianism by his mother's ethics, Gandhi found himself in the land of the English breakfast, a robust meal that featured at least two forms of red meat when worthy of its name. England was the home of the London broil, the meat pie, and the mutton chop. A commonly-held belief among the English was that a vegetarian diet would make one weak and puny. As an achingly young expat, Gandhi was worried they might be right.

Gandhi's interest in vegetarianism was quite secondhand. He was, at best, a nominal Hindu at this point in his life. He had never taken a serious interest in the sacred texts of his religion. His faith took the form of compliance with its external tokens and rituals. His mother was a truly spiritual person, for whom religion was the basis of life, and he loved and respected his mother. He was determined to remain vegetarian, not because he believed in it but because he had promised Putlibai he would. And while he was not yet a deeply religious man, he was truthful and determined not to break his word.

So the young Mohandas scoped out and located a couple of vegetarian restaurants. At the modest Central, he found an unassuming handbill by Henry Stephens Salt, entitled "A Plea for Vegetarianism." Gandhi read it and was inspired. It was the first of many Western texts that would illuminate Indian and Hindu practices for Gandhi and help form the philosophical basis for his life of action and self-sacrifice.

If one sees Gandhi's early life as a series of dominoes falling toward the liberation of India from English rule, his visit to the Central and his reading of "A Plea for Vegetarianism" represented the first domino to fall.

Through his reading of "A Plea for Vegetarianism," Gandhi became friends with Salt, its author, and that friendship led to a happy association with the Vegetarian Society, which in turn led to association with the English Theosophists, the Simple Lifers, and the Esoteric Christians. Gandhi went to London mostly alone, shy, poor, and friendless, but through his promise to his mother to avoid meat, he soon found himself at the center of numerous intersecting intellectual circles— informal collections of people who were asking the kinds of questions he was asking: What is the role of God in the world? Where do we find purpose? What is our responsibility to our fellow man? To our fellow creatures?

How, you might ask, did a young Hindu end up so far from home? Mohandas was born in 1869 in Porbandar, India. His family was influential and politically connected. His father held the title of provincial prime minister, a title that had been handed down from Mohandas' grandfather. The Gandhis belonged to the **Vaishyas**, a middle-ranking Hindu caste that had originally been peopled by farmers but expanded to include merchants and traders. The India of Gandhi's birth was a mixture of religions and sharp social and economic disparities. Hindus were the majority, but the Muslim minority was generally wealthier and more powerful.

Mohandas was the youngest child of his father's fourth wife. His early education in India was typical of the time and place to which he was born. He was a mediocre student, apparently excelling at nothing in particular. He did like poetry and stories, the more allegorical or mythological the better. He was particularly enamored of the tales of King Harishchandra, a hero of HInduism who told the truth at all costs, even when moral relativism would have spared his loved ones great pain.

Gandhi's education was interrupted for a year after his arranged marriage to a fellow child, Kasturbai. The bride was fourteen and the groom thirteen when they tied the knot. Such child marriages were the custom in India. In the early years of their marriage, their tie was a loose one. They only lived together half the year, returning home to live as children in their respective parents' homes for the remainder. Despite what might appear to some a thin commitment, the couple had a child together at a very young age, and Gandhi was a father before he started law school. Though there were several obstacles to Gandhi's journey to England, his marriage and consequent separation from his wife for several years were, amazingly, never floated as an objection.

Despite his less-than-stellar academic achievements and his low status in the pecking order of multiple wives and children, Mohandas was identified as the right candidate to inherit his father's post as regional prime minister—a post that, as events transpired, he would never actually hold. But an English law degree was a necessary stepping stone. The family's limited financial resources posed a problem, but some of Kasturbai's jewelry was sold to finance the trip and the years abroad. Mohandas' extended family and more religious members of the community also kicked up a fuss. They regarded a sojourn in England as a form of heresy, a betrayal of Hindu belief.

To some extent, Mohandas' mother shared the belief that an English education would compromise Mohandas' soul. The solution was for her son to take a solemn vow to observe the important Hindu prohibitions. That vow was chiefly what propelled Gandhi to the vegetarian restaurant that catalyzed his political thinking.

At the time of Gandhi's birth, English rule in India was an established fact, one that seemed impossible to challenge. The official reason for English interference in India was the "white man's burden," a belief that the British had a duty to bring their form of government and moral norms to "less civilized" parts of the world. The unofficial reason for England's occupation of India was to tap Indian resources to expand British wealth while making a further profit through the export of goods, like fabrics, to India.

It is important to note that the British colonists did not, by and large, see themselves as self-centered profit mongers, especially not in the first decades of their occupation. By their own account, they were neither invaders nor tyrants. And many Indians participated in the belief that a British-governed India was a good thing. It is customary for twenty-first century readers to see British colonization as an entirely ego-driven, culture-blind form of arrogance. However, we must recognize that the British did bring a few reforms to India. They quickly outlawed suttee, the practice of murdering a widowed woman shortly after the death of her husband. The

British, under the leadership of William Bentinck, also managed to end the murderous regime of the Thuggees, a roving gang of Indian **assassins** who specialized in robbing and murdering caravan travelers.

So the British were not clear-cut villains in the story to which Mohandas Gandhi was born. To be sure, the British treated Indians like children, made no real attempt to understand Indian history or religion, and arrogantly assumed that their relatively new civilization was better than one that had hundreds of years on them. But the British ruled in India for nearly a century at least in part because Indians themselves were ambivalent about British rule.

Gandhi himself couldn't wait to get to England. He frequently felt oppressed by the suffocating intimacy of a big family and a close-knit community. And though he had shown only a middling aptitude for scholastics, he had an inquiring mind. When he arrived in England, Gandhi was an almost perfect representative of Indian ambivalence toward British rule in India. He understood that the British contempt for Indian religion made them unfit to rule such a religious country, but he had, up to that point, taken little real interest in his own religion. He could see the beauty of the British emphasis on individuality and freedom while he also recognized that such emphasis could result in disconnection and loneliness. He brought his native Indian clothes with him and, while on the ship, ate almost entirely out of his own stockpile of Hindu-compliant foods. But upon his arrival in London, he quickly exchanged his native garb for the suit, tie, and top hat of a "proper" English gentleman.

Gandhi found little to admire in jolly old meat-eating, fox-hunting, cricket-loving mainstream England, but the small societies of radical, sometimes even fringe, thinkers to which his vegetarian lunch at the Central led galvanized him. He became an official member of the International Vegetarian Union. Through that membership and his friendship with Salt, he met *Daily Telegraph* editor Edwin Arnold, vegetarian writer Anna Kingsford, and Theosophy founder Annie Besant.

Gandhi made the acquaintance of Josiah Oldfield, who edited *The Vegetarian*, and became a contributor to that magazine for many years. One of his earliest contributions was an informative, five-part series on Indian vegetarianism. For the most part, this set of articles was a simple overview of vegetarianism as practiced in India. Gandhi explained that only members of the Brahmin and Vaishya castes were expected to be vegetarian. They consumed milk because milking a cow does not harm her, but they abstained from eating eggs, which are potentially living creatures. Yet even in these early essays, Gandhi revealed a keen political worldview—an ability to set an issue against its larger socio-economic backdrop. He noted that many Indians were not vegetarians because of religious belief, but because of poverty, and he briefly complained about the exorbitant salt tax, which became an important talking point in his later campaign to liberate India from British rule.

Perhaps more importantly than the people he met were the authors he read while in London. Though he had never distinguished himself as a student, in London he became a voracious reader who somehow balanced the full-time study of law with an extracurricular reading agenda that prepared him to become a revolutionary world leader. Most people accept book recommendations unenthusiastically with vague promises and, later, mumbled excuses. Gandhi, by contrast, would accept a book from a friend, read it cover to cover, and carefully place it within the emerging framework of his political and spiritual ideology. Even if, from his point of view, a book was nonsense, he would read enough of it to make sure. He found kindred spirits in a diverse set of writers and freethinkers that included the poet Percy B. Shelley, Thomas Carlyle, George Bernard Shaw, Cardinal Manning, John Ruskin, and Walt Whitman. Many of the books that he read as a very young London exile no longer have much name recognition, but they were on the cutting edge of progressive thought at that time. One writer who has endured the test of time, Henry David Thoreau, was extremely influential on Gandhi's thinking. Thoreau's *Walden* resonated strongly with the Simple Life movement with which Gandhi became loosely associated. And it would be a mistake to underestimate the long-term effect that reading Thoreau's *Civil Disobedience* had on the evolution of passive resistance.

Ironically, it was not until a couple of new friends recommended it that Gandhi read the great Hindu text, the Bhagavad Gita, as translated into English by Edwin Arnold. Because it was written to fill in the blanks for non-Hindus, Arnold's translation was actually more cohesive and therefore more useful to Gandhi than the original text was. In the Gita, Gandhi found the same concerns that preoccupied him. The central question that the book tries to answer is "What are we for?" The Hindu belief in salvation through action took hold in Gandhi for the first time as he read the English translation of the ancient and sacred text.

Another unlikely road that led Gandhi to a newfound value for Hinduism was his reading of Madame Blavatsky's book *Key to Theosophy*. The cornerstone of Theosophy, Blavatsky's text is a blend of religious ecumenism and science fiction. It puts forward the noble ideal of universal brotherhood and the sensible idea that all religions are seeking truth. The book also dabbles in telepathy and spirit channeling. Though it achieved little traction in history, the *Key to Theosophy* does praise the Hindu faith as being superior to other, more structured religions.

Like many young men who take for granted the privileges of their youth and upbringing, Gandhi had placed little value on the riches of the religion in which he was raised. But when he saw the greatness of the Hindu faith through Western eyes, his own eyes were opened. Many of the ideas that Gandhi absorbed in London—the purity of a vegetarian diet, the virtues of simplicity, the evils of clamoring for material possessions, religion as a bridge to truth rather than a set of strictures—remained forever on the fringe of British culture, but these ideas would find a richer, more fertile field in India, which was already culturally attuned and receptive to such ideas.

In the long run, the many activities that distracted Gandhi from the full-time study of law—his forays into writing, his attendance at parties and meetings with freethinkers, and his reading of books that were not remotely related to the law— would prove much more relevant to his lifetime work than would his law degree. Nevertheless, he kept up his official studies, rarely failed an important test, and was "called to the bar" in June of 1891, meaning he had earned his lawyer's credential. Two days later, he sailed for India and home, but he was not the same unpromising, middle-of-the-road young man who had left for London three years earlier. The books he had read, the people he had met, and the ideas in which he had steeped himself for three years had transformed him.

Lawyer to activist

He stood up to
racism and fought
for his right

they through him out
of a train

they feel him 3rd not
first class

He was waiting for
his own right

There's no reason not to think that Gandhi might eventually have made an adequate lawyer, but his imagination and relentless search for the truth combined with historical circumstances to pave a much broader destiny than that of the competent urban attorney.

Things had changed by the time he returned to India. His mother had died just a few months before his return. His family had deliberately withheld the news of her death from Mohandas. They had wished to spare him the distraction from his studies at a critical juncture in his career. The family's political influence had also diminished since the death of Gandhi's father. Several family members had lost their government jobs; their connections and social influence had waned. Mohandas Gandhi was no longer in line to inherit the prime minister position that his father had held.

So the 21-year-old lawyer went to Bombay, where he set up a small, independent law practice. It was not a success. He arrived in the big city at a time when Bombay was flooded with lawyers, more than were needed to meet market demands. New lawyers in general could find work only through referrals from other lawyers or from friends and family members. But Gandhi was poorly connected in

Bombay. His friends and family back in Porbandar were of no help in sending clients.

Despite these serious obstacles, Mohandas might have succeeded. He was young, smart, energetic, and sociable. But he refused to resort to a shady practice that spelled success for many Bombay lawyers. Specifically, he refused to hire a "tout." Touts were basically ambulance chasers who were hired and sent out in the city to hunt potential litigation and then bring it back to the law office. The legal profession in Bombay officially recognized that this ambulance chasing was unethical; but, unofficially, it was rampant. Gandhi unequivocally refused to hire touts. Even when associates pointed out that he was choosing poverty and failure over ethics, he stood fast. For him, it was never really a choice.

After a short spell doing paralegal work for his brother, who was a more successful lawyer, Gandhi accepted a position with Dada Abdulla and Company, an Indian company doing business in South Africa. The firm took its name from its founder and owner, Dada Abdulla, a wealthy Muslim who had gone to South Africa to make his fortune and succeeded. At the time that Gandhi joined his firm, Abdulla was the owner of an international shipping company and two trading houses.

The job he offered Gandhi entailed moving to South Africa and assisting the company's team of lawyers to win a case involving a disputed sum of 40,000 British pounds, a small fortune in that era. It was not a prestigious position, but it did offer Mohandas an escape from the drudgery of clerical work and the unenviable position of poor relation in his brother's practice.

South Africa in Gandhi's time was not kind to Indians despite the fact that Muslim entrepreneurs accounted for a huge part of its gross national product. The Indian population was sharply divided into two widely disparate classes: the wealthy business owners, who controlled much of the country's economy, and laborers, who were indentured or formerly indentured. The wealthy Indians looked down on their fellow countrymen in the laboring class. In the eyes of Dutch and British white men, however, all Indians were lowlifes. The slurs "coolie" and "sammy" (corrupted from "swami") were bandied about freely and applied to all Indians, regardless of status or wealth.

Dada Abdulla, Mohandas' new boss, met Gandhi at the port where he arrived and gave him a quick tour of the Natal province, where Abdulla lived and worked. One of Gandhi's first assignments was to appear in court as a company representative. He showed up in the gear of an Englishman—a tailored suit with well-heeled and polished shoes—but he topped off this modern ensemble with the turban he traditionally wore. The judge told him in no uncertain terms to remove it, at which point Gandhi left the courtroom.

Gandhi was inclined, however, not to make a long-term issue of the turban. He told Abdulla what had transpired and indicated that he would be willing to wear a more English-looking hat instead. Abdulla, however, gave the first indication that he would become an important advocate for social change: he instructed Gandhi to hold the line and retain his turban because it was a point on which Indians across the Natal had agreed to push back.

Soon it was time for Gandhi to pack his bags and take a trip across the Natal. He had been hired to assist in prosecuting a specific case, and the case was being heard in Pretoria. Abdulla paid all of Gandhi's travel expenses to his new post—which included a first-class train ticket. What the company failed to mention in their correspondence was that, in South Africa, the railway system could legally deny any Indian his purchased first-class seat. Gandhi's train ride across Africa would be a merciless and grueling baptism in South Africa's mistreatment of its Indian population.

Mohandas Gandhi's identification with all men, no matter how poor or low-born, was a work in progress. It would be several decades before he would champion the cause of the untouchables and insist on boarding in the poorest accommodations when traveling. The young man who boarded the train for the first leg of his Pretoria journey was well-dressed and English-educated, and he had no problem with traveling first class while his fellow countrymen crowded into less amenable parts of the train. But his unconscious privilege was soon to be shattered.

The train stopped at a station, and a white passenger entered the car where Gandhi was seated. Instead of taking his seat, the new passenger immediately turned and located a station manager who told Gandhi that, because he was a "coolie," he would have to retire to the third-class compartment. Gandhi politely declined and showed the manager his first-class ticket, at which point, more staff were summoned and

Mohandas was summarily thrown off the train. As the train huffed away, the well-dressed young lawyer stood on the platform, bewildered. The night was dark, and the station was cold, but there he passed the night. Gandhi sent a telegram to Abdulla, who managed to get him on another train, but the journey was still far from over and far from offering no further drama.

From Charlestown to Johannesburg, the only available transportation was a stage-coach. Here, too, Mohandas encountered flagrant racism. A white man, much bigger than Gandhi, informed him that he would have to ride on the outside of the carriage; then he tried to make Gandhi dangle precariously on the coach's footboard. When Gandhi refused, the man attempted to drag him physically out of his seat. Finally, he bowed to the protests of the other paying customers who begged him to stop harassing the young lawyer.

In Johannesburg, Gandhi found that he was unable to book into a hotel. The attendant informed him that it was "full," though it was obviously not. All along this journey, Gandhi met and chatted with other Indians who assured him that this rough treatment was business as usual. Some of them expressed surprise that he was so naive as to think that he could travel first-class or check into a hotel at will.

The last leg of his journey took him by train, again, to Pretoria. By this time, his activist instincts were fully ignited. His peers told him that in Dutch-controlled Johannesburg, he would not even be allowed to buy a first-class ticket. However, Gandhi made a point of reading the railway's regulatory fine print. Nowhere did it say that an Indian could not purchase a first-class ticket. So Mohandas sent a written notice to the station master, stating that he was a lawyer and expected to travel first class. When he followed this up in person, he got his ticket. There was a tense moment when a guard once again tried to make him move to another car, but his fellow passenger spoke up and said he did "not mind" sharing the compartment with an Indian.

Natal Indian Congress

Immediately upon his arrival in Pretoria, a couple of Christian communities—a group of Quakers and a few Plymouth brethren—befriended the 23-year-old lawyer. Gandhi returned their friendly overtures, and they stayed on friendly terms throughout his time in Africa. But the Christianity taught by these folk did not resonate with Gandhi as would the Christian ideology of Leo Tolstoy or even the Esoteric Christianity with which he would soon rub shoulders. Gandhi could not easily relate to the notion of a quick and easy forgiveness that put no real pressure on the individual to improve himself. He adamantly believed in self-improvement. One of the Plymouth brethren tactlessly told Gandhi that he should destroy a Hindu ornament representing Vaishnava that he wore on his neck, on the grounds that it was superstitious. In delivering this polemic, the brother showed no sensitivity to the fact that the ornament was a gift from Gandhi's beloved late mother.

His disastrous train ride had turned Gandhi into an activist, and he lost no time in rallying the Indian community to demand reforms. Within a week of his arrival in Pretoria, he called a meeting of his fellow countrymen to discuss what should be done. In arranging this meeting, he enlisted an unlikely ally: Tyeb Sheth. Sheth was the very adversary against whom Abdulla had filed suit. Sheth was deeply embedded in the Pretoria Indian community, and Gandhi quickly realized that he would make little headway without Sheth's help. It must have taken considerable tact to approach Sheth for help in the Indian cause whilst also prosecuting a case against him, but somehow Gandhi pulled it off.

The meeting came to pass, and Gandhi gave a speech, his first as an activist. In the Bombay courts, he had been tentative and lacked confidence as a speaker, but in Africa he immediately found his voice. He made no attempt to engage his audience with wit or humor. He engaged them with ideas and with the seriousness of his commitment to change. He asked them to do their part—to learn English, to be scrupulously honest in business, to observe good hygiene, and to desist from sectarian bickering. Failure to do so lowered them in the eyes of the white man, he noted. That meeting gave birth to other meetings. As the years passed, Gandhi would become the face of Indian revolt against Dutch and British injustice in South Africa.

Though he quickly established himself as a leader in obtaining better treatment for the Indian community, Gandhi did not neglect the mission for which he was employed. He carefully

studied the case of *Abdulla* v. *Sheth* and concluded that
Abdulla had justice on his side. However, he could also see
that this lawsuit threatened to drain the resources of both
litigants disastrously. Both parties were bitter and not
thinking rationally.

Gandhi, with the peace-making talent for which he would
become a legend, found a win-win solution. He got both
parties to agree to binding arbitration that would resolve
their dispute quickly and cheaply. The arbitrator found in
favor of Abdulla and charged Seth to pay 37,000 pounds plus
court costs. It was a sum that would have utterly ruined Seth,
even if he had been able to pay the full amount, which he was
not. Gandhi briefly worried that Seth might commit suicide
rather than face the disgrace of an unpaid debt. So once again,
he stepped in, and he persuaded Abdulla to let Seth pay him in
installments over a long period of time. Word of Abdulla's
compassion traveled and improved the trader's prestige. It
was, all around, the best solution to an ugly conflict.

Once Gandhi had settled this dispute, he was free to devote
himself more fully to the plight of Indians in South Africa.
There was plenty to complain about. Indians in South Africa
were not only prohibited from traveling first class; they were

also subject to a curfew that forbade them to be out of their houses after 9 p.m. And they were even prohibited from walking on the sidewalks.

One day, Gandhi picked up a newspaper and read that legislation had been introduced to deny Indians the right to vote. He and his fellows launched a campaign against this effort. Though he was ultimately unsuccessful and the legislation was passed, Gandhi demonstrated his leadership ability when he caused a delay in the form of a Colony Secretary's veto.

The Indian community did not hesitate to identify Gandhi as a promising leader. With his usual high-mindedness, he would accept no payment for his work as a reformist and social advocate. So a group of Indian businessmen got together and offered him retainers, which provided him with an annual income of 300 pounds—sufficient for him to live on. Officially, Gandhi was retained to serve as their legal advisor. Unofficially, he was now in Africa to better the lives of Indians living and working there.

Informal meetings of his countrymen paved the way for Gandhi to establish a more formal body, called the Natal

Indian Congress, of which he was the first secretary. The new organization was modeled on the Indian National Congress back in India, an organization that sought better rights for home Indians under British rule. The Natal Indian Congress met regularly, though not on a set schedule; sometimes it met once a week, sometimes once in a month.

Part of Gandhi's mission was to give his countrymen the tools to fight for their cause peacefully. That meant they needed to read and sharpen their rhetorical skills. The congress opened a library and a debating society. During this period, Gandhi wrote and published two pamphlets that obtained an international readership. One was titled *An Appeal to Every Briton in South Africa*. This treatise frankly exposed the deplorable status and treatment of Natal Indians. The other pamphlet was titled *The Indian Franchise—An Appeal*, and it related the history of the Indian franchise in Natal. Both works found their way to England and infiltrated British sentiment. It is probably no coincidence that the *Times* of London published eight in-depth articles exposing the problems of Natal Indians over the next eight years.

S.S. Courland and the Green Pamphlet

ss courland was a
brit ship

the green pamphlet
is a book about how
the brits treat the indeans
in South affrica

Gandhi kept up a polite association with the local Christians, though he kept them at an emotional and spiritual distance. Their message and rituals—singing to an organ on Sundays, tea, and polite conversation—seemed limited and uninspirational. This did not, however, mean that he rejected Christianity as a model for political and social transformation.

Two books came along—both of them set within a Christian framework—that would become building blocks in his ideology. One was *The Kingdom of Heaven Is Within You* by the nineteenth-century novelist Leo Tolstoy—better known as the author of *War and Peace*. Tolstoy was a Russian abolitionist who freed his own serfs. In his book, he argued that God is within everyone and that the secret to happiness is to quit seeking material gain and, instead, to give up one's material possessions. Tolstoy also positioned the Christian as a revolutionary and a disruptor, someone who is willing to defy immoral laws and confront authority at great risk to himself. It's fairly easy to see how this train of thought could shape a man who, years later, would believe in martyrdom as the first line of defense and give up wearing anything but a one-piece loin cloth.

Another book that Gandhi read early in his South African adventure was *The Perfect Way* by Anna Kingsford. This book, which has failed to withstand the test of time, is a theosophical take on Christianity, which finds in the Christian faith the rationale for vegetarianism and meditation that were dear to the author. It may be difficult for modern readers to see how Gandhi could be so inspired by a book that, from an historical perspective, fell by the wayside. To understand why the *Perfect Way* was so important to Gandhi, however, we need to appreciate the book's ability to demonstrate plainly how faith and thought can be transformed directly into compassionate action and a lifestyle of self-abnegation. These were the ideas that consistently mobilized Gandhi—wherever they came from. *The Perfect Way* and *The Kingdom of Heaven Is Within You* were the philosophical platform for Gandhi's strategies of martyrdom and civil disobedience.

Several of Gandhi's early campaigns in South Africa were unsuccessful. He ultimately failed to protect the Indian vote. Similarly, he and the congress failed to stop the passage of legislation that limited new Indian immigration and trade in South Africa. However, he quickly made a name for himself. South African officials all knew who he was, as did many politicians in England, and they trembled to think what he would do next. Even before he had accomplished any real reforms, Gandhi was recognized far and wide as a threat to white supremacy—so much so that, upon returning to Africa from a trip to India, he was refused readmission to the country.

Gandhi was returning to South Africa aboard the S.S. *Courland*. He had traveled back to India specifically to report on the condition of Indian rights in Africa. His Indian trip was cut short when activists back in Africa sent him an urgent message to return at once. However, Gandhi's return voyage passed through a terrible storm, and Gandhi was one of the few passengers who kept his calm throughout, doing what he could to help the other passengers. The ship's crew were impressed. When the ship docked in Durban, the passengers all expected to disembark and put the terrible ship ride behind them. But that was not what happened.

Government authorities refused to allow the ship's passengers to disembark. They cited a pneumonia outbreak in Bombay prior to the ship's departure. But everyone knew the real reason: white leaders were furious with Gandhi over his most recent publication, the Green Pamphlet—a book that, in no uncertain terms, condemned the British treatment of Indians in South Africa. The book's official title was *The Grievances of the British Indians in South Africa: An Appeal to the Indian Public,* but because of its green cover and its grassroots popularity, it became more commonly known by its colorful nickname.

Gandhi had written and published the Green Pamphlet on his visit to India, and with the assistance of neighborhood children, he personally handled its distribution before leaving India. In the pamphlet, he summarized human rights violations about which he had written in other articles. The pamphlet cited the experience of Abdulla Haji Adam, an Indian ship owner operating in Africa. On a trip to Natal, this individual had alighted at Krantzkloof Station to get a bite to eat. However, because of his ethnicity, no one would sell him anything edible, not even a slice of plain bread. The local hotelier likewise refused him a room, forcing him to overnight in an unheated coach during a bleak, cold winter month. The Green Pamphlet also called attention to the recently passed Immigration Bill of 1894. The very text of this bill openly admitted that the purpose of its authors was to make Indians more comfortable in India than in the Natal colony of South Africa.

Gandhi's observations about the plight of Indians were accurate and, if anything, understated, but media reports on the book skewed its message. In London, Reuters reported the Green Pamphlet as claiming that Indians were being randomly assaulted and treated like animals.

The passengers on the *Courland* insisted on their right to disembark, so a stalemate ensued that lasted 23 days. The *Courland*'s crew and travelers spent Christmas and New Year's Day stuck on the docked ship. When one medical officer declared that it was safe to let the passengers leave the ship, he was quickly replaced with another medical officer, who lengthened the quarantine. The stasis of the *Courland* made possible a proliferation of gossip and meetings that meant no good for Gandhi. One of the wildest rumors afoot was that the *Courland* was carrying a printing press and fifty professionals trained in the science of printing. The goal of this cargo, so the rumor went, was to launch a full-throated campaign for an increase in Indian immigration. Another rumor that garnered traction was that Gandhi was preparing to establish an emigration agency that would bring up to two thousand new Indians per month to South Africa.

There was no merit to any of these wild accusations. Except for his immediate family members, the passengers aboard the Courland had no professional or personal relationship to Gandhi. Many of them were bound for points beyond the ship's landing. These same passengers were, however, hungry, thirsty, and desperately in need of a change of clothes. Many of them had gotten drenched during the storm crossing. The ship's captain was unable to disembark, so he sent an SOS signal from the ship asking for clothes and blankets. The signal was directed to local government authorities, who paid it no heed whatsoever. Fortunately, however, the Indian community also saw the SOS. They responded more kindly by sending free food to help the ship's poorest passengers, and they also sent enough blankets for all of the passengers.

When it was no longer possible to pretend that the ship's passengers could infect the general public with pneumonia, they were allowed to leave the ship. Gandhi was well aware that an angry mob awaited him at the port. Therefore, he sent his wife and two sons quietly ashore under the cover of night. He himself was advised to do the same, but he opted to leave the ship in broad daylight and use the gangplank.

A mixed mob awaited him on shore. Some of them had come to regard Gandhi as a saint. Others wanted him dead. His fans sent up a chant of "Gandhi! Gandhi!" They were, however, far outnumbered by an angry collection of white people, who assaulted him, tore off his turban, and proceeded to beat him. Amidst shouted curses and threats, Gandhi found himself pelted with jagged brick pieces, stones, mud, and rotten fish. One man lashed him with a whip. He could remain standing only by propping himself up on the railing of a nearby house. In his memoirs, Gandhi would write that he did not expect to reach home alive.

In the spirit of passive resistance, he did nothing to defend himself. He did not raise a hand against his attackers. He might well have been killed except that the wife of the local police superintendent came to his aid. Armed only with an open parasol, which she used as a shield, she protected him until the police arrived. That night, the same mob surrounded Gandhi's home, shouting "Hang old Gandhi on the sour apple tree!" The police superintendent who was posted outside the house for Gandhi's safety happily joined in the chant.

To protect his family, Gandhi was finally persuaded to leave the house out the back door and make his way to the police station. He donned the disguise of an Indian constable, and two white detectives made themselves up to look like Indian merchants. Under this guard, Gandhi was safely escorted to the police station.

It took quite a while for the police superintendent to convince the crowd to disperse. They threatened to set fire to the house if the police did not hand Gandhi over to them. When the superintendent noted that Gandhi's wife and children were in the house, the crowd reiterated its intention to burn the house down. Finally, the superintendent was able to convince the mob to send in a team of three or four men to ascertain for themselves that Gandhi was not at home. That worked, and the disappointed crowd finally dispersed.

For his own safety, Gandhi spent two nights in the police station. Afterward, many people, including Colonial Secretary Chamberlain, urged him to press charges against his attackers. He refused to do so. In his memoirs, Gandhi would refer to this episode as "The Test." Though there were many such tests and hardships to come, this was perhaps the first opportunity to show exactly how committed to non-violence he really was and how prepared he was to sacrifice his own life in a just cause. In the near future, he would ask his followers to do the same. He himself passed the test—with flying colors.

In 1900, Gandhi took a break from social activism on behalf of Indian rights to serve the British Empire. The Boer War had erupted, and it pitted the British against the Dutch in a battle for sovereignty and territory. Gandhi found himself somewhat torn. To some degree, he sympathized with the Dutch Boers, but he was technically a British citizen, and he had not yet evolved in his thinking to the point where he wished to relinquish that identity. So he found a way to support the British without compromising his values of peace and non-violence toward every living creature: he persuaded the British armed forces to train and deploy an all-Indian ambulance corps.

He encountered some initial resistance in this because the British saw Indians as shifty and unreliable. But as the war dragged on, the Brits could hardly afford to turn down this noble offer. Three hundred free Indians, along with eight hundred who were still indentured, formed this platoon. They worked tirelessly, marching as much as twenty miles a day. At the battle of Spion Kop, motorized vehicles could not access the wounded because of the rugged terrain, so Gandhi's corps carried the wounded for miles across hostile ground to the nearest field hospital. They received numerous verbal accolades, with one military leader noting that they had succeeded where British troops would have withered from the heat and the lack of food and water. Thirty-seven of this group as well as Gandhi received medals honoring their service. With characteristic optimism, Gandhi overestimated the value of these honors and compliments. He somewhat naively believed that a new day had dawned for Indians in South Africa and that the British would now be obliged to recognize them as equals. He was mistaken. In the long-term, the British crackdown on Indians only worsened.

The Indian Opinion

He starts a newspaper
and starts

By 1903, Gandhi had clearly realized the power of the written word to create awareness and mobilize masses. So it's no real surprise that he chose to leverage his talents by starting up a newspaper to create awareness about the treatment of Indians in South Africa. That newspaper was titled the *Indian Opinion*. It supported the work of the Natal Indian Congress and underlined future campaigns for equal rights. The *Indian Opinion* maintained a measured, respectful tone, free of hysteria and exaggeration. It is important to note that it did not call for the British to leave Africa or India. Gandhi was, at this point in his career, still clinging to vestiges of faith in British culture and civilization.

However, the *Opinion* did report on instances of abuses: employers assaulting indentured servants, for instance, and the high suicide rate amongst Indians in Africa. Simultaneously, the *Indian Opinion* heralded the actions of those who peacefully resisted abuse. The paper also published poetry that celebrated "satyagraha," the term that Gandhi coined to describe non-violent non-cooperation. In fact, Gandhi declared that satyagraha would have been "impossible" without the support of the *Opinion*.

It is worthwhile to pause in our story to define 'satyagraha,' both as Gandhi defined it and as it was used in campaigns to liberate Indians in South Africa and, later, in India. Satyagraha was always more than martyrdom. The underlying premise of satyagraha was that the world is a stage and civil disobedience is a drama acted out on that stage. Every satyagraha involves a villain, which was usually the British oppressor, sometimes the Dutch. But the main players are those who purposely break an unfair law to make a point. For satyagraha to work, there must always be an audience, who must be convinced, for the most part, that the lawbreaker is a righteous hero. The audience then condemns the villain as a bully. This drama continues until the villain himself finally comes to see himself as a bully and desists from his villainy. The heroes of satyagraha must be volunteers who joyfully give themselves over to beatings, possible murder, and frequent imprisonment. Because satyagraha requires a public stage and an audience, it must be carefully planned out. It is never conducted as a surprise attack. The villains of the story must always be given ample notice so that they can play their parts in the drama.

One particularly interesting twist on satyagraha as Gandhi practiced it was to avoid taking advantage of any weakness in the opponent that resulted from other conflicts. For instance, when the British turned their attention to war, Gandhi would typically put satyagraha on hold so as not to exploit the British while they were distracted with another conflict.

Many social scientists have critiqued satyagraha. Some have offered the opinion that it only worked against the British because the British recognized certain boundaries of decency that benefited the independence movement. A number of historians have proposed that satyagraha cannot work in a completely despotic state where those who challenge authority simply disappear or are found murdered before they can achieve anything remotely resembling a following. Gandhi, himself, however, believed in the universal application of satyagraha. During Hitler's massacre of Europe's Jews, Gandhi said that the Jews should find a way to publicly offer themselves up to the violence of their oppressor. Note the importance, in his thinking, of the stage and audience.

Satyagraha was the unifying theme of Gandhi's life. And the *Indian Opinion* gave him a vehicle in which to develop these ideas at length and show how they applied to a shifting political landscape. Hebert Kitchin, Henry Polak, Albert West, Gandhi's daughter-in-law Sushila Gandhi, and Gandhi's son Manilal Gandhi were, at various points, editors of the paper.

The *Indian Opinion* was born to blur the line between journalism and social action. All of its editors were activists. All but one was imprisoned for political resistance.

There was never any suggestion that the *Indian Opinion* should be run as a business or turn a profit. That was not its purpose. It was, in fact, a drain on the financial resources of the campaign for better Indian rights. Early in the life of the *Indian Opinion*, a staff member complained to Gandhi that the paper was literally hemorrhaging money. Gandhi's solution was to move the newspaper, printer and all, to a rural cooperative, peopled by Indian and European followers attuned to his philosophy.

So he placed an advertisement for land and got a nibble. This led to the purchase of one hundred acres, fourteen miles outside Durban, for around one thousand pounds. The farm contained a single cottage in disrepair, a spring, and fruit trees. It held the promise of being farmable even though even though only a few acres had been turned over. The rest was snake-infested wild grass. Nevertheless, this land would form the location of Gandhi's first ashram, one of many experiments in communal living to which he devoted himself.

Gandhi moved himself and his family there. The first task was to build a small warehouse for the printing press. Luckily, a Parsee man who was friendly to Gandhi's efforts donated an allotment of corrugated iron. Within a month, the family had built a structure seventy-five feet in length and fifty feet in width. The ashramites themselves lived in canvas tents until they were able to build small houses out of the same iron material.

At the height of its success, the Phoenix Settlement, as it came to be called, housed six families. The main work of this cooperative was to produce the newspaper, but residents also collaborated in raising and educating children, and they dabbled in growing bananas. Each resident received a stipend of three pounds a month.

The newspaper itself proved a technological challenge. To lower printing costs, Gandhi initially proposed using a hand press, but that quickly proved impractical. An oil-run printer was brought in, but the engine broke, so it had to be hand-cranked in shifts by the cooperative's residents. Eventually, four local Zulu women were hired to keep the press rolling.

Life at the Phoenix was austere. It was an experiment in voluntary simplicity, a concept to which Gandhi would increasingly commit himself and those who followed him. He was already washing and starching his own clothes, however haphazardly, and cutting his own hair. Unsympathetic observers thought he'd been nibbled at by rats, but their jeers meant nothing to him. If they upheld superficial, materialistic values, that was very much their problem. The twin concepts of self-reliance and doing without had achieved a shimmering beauty in Gandhi's eyes.

Phoenix residents rose early in the morning and wore simple non-Western clothes. On Sunday evenings, the flock enjoyed readings from the Bible and the Bhagavad Gita. At one point, however, two of the residents fell from grace. It's impossible to know exactly how they strayed from what Gandhi considered a righteous path, but their infraction distressed him to the degree that he jumped on a train out of Johannesburg to come straight back to the farm. There he "punished" the wayward residents by starving himself for a week. In many ways, this small action foreshadowed the greater events in which Gandhi had a hand. In years to come, he would embrace harm to himself, and encourage others to do the same, in order to shame the British oppressor.

In 1906, Gandhi took his now-famous vow of celibacy, sometimes referred to as *brahmacharya*. In Hindi, *brahmacharya* simply means "self-control," but in Gandhi's world, it came to mean abstinence from sex. Gandhi did not arrive at this decision impulsively but, rather, discussed the issue with friends and followers. His main objective in renouncing sex was to commit himself more fully to religiously-infused social action. He has been criticized for not consulting his wife, Kasturbai, before making up his mind, but it is worth noting that she never complained about the decision.

In the same year, Gandhi once again set aside his conflict with the British, this time because the British were preoccupied with an uprising of the Zulu people. Gandhi offered to organize another ambulance corps, and his offer was accepted by the Natal governor, who remembered how well the Indians had served in the Boer War. The Zulu had assassinated two British officers in reaction to a new poll tax. Gandhi believed in this undertaking because he bought into the British representation: the lawless, violent Zulu were randomly murdering government representatives.

When Gandhi and his colleagues got in the field, however, they quickly realized that the Zulu were unarmed, most of them offered little or no resistance, and the British picked them off with no questions asked. As a consequence, Gandhi's corps spent more of its energy tending to wounded Zulus who had been shot or whipped. The Zulus were the only ones who needed medical attention, and many of the wounded had nothing to do with the minor rebellion. Gandhi's corps of 24 uniformed medical personnel were the only ones who lifted a hand to help the battered Zulus. As Gandhi's medical unit hastened to provide aid, British soldiers jeered at them and used hateful slurs to describe the Black Africans. British actions horrified Gandhi, who found new reasons to oppose British rule and who also now believed that the British could only be persuaded by civil disobedience.

Fingerprints

He protested peacfully.

the Tara act was put in place
So indians had to get all ten
finger prints they protested to
end this act and Gandi went to
Jail several times

In 1907 the *Indian Opinion* would be an important instrument in resisting new legislation that would force many Indians to submit to fingerprinting and random home inspections. Then, in 1906, a new bill required all Indians in the Transvaal to re-register. Whereas they had previously been allowed to register with a signature or, in the case of those who could not write, a simple thumbprint, now the Transvaal Asiatic Registration Act (TARA) required ten fingerprints. The law applied to all Indians in South Africa over the age of eight, both men and women. Concurrently, the law, nicknamed the Black Law by the Indian community, permitted policemen to enter Indian homes at will and interrogate wives and mothers.

It may be difficult for the twenty-first century western mind to understand the outrage that this caused the Indian community, so it is important to understand the historical and cultural context. At this time, only criminals were fully fingerprinted. The new law, therefore, put all Indians, no matter how successful or law abiding, on a par with felons. Furthermore, the suggestion that a stranger could, with impunity, approach a married woman in her home in the absence of her husband or father was a terrible insult to the religious sensitivities of most traditional Indians.

Gandhi took a stand, addressing the Natal Indian Congress in no uncertain terms. His audience was more than ready to resist this new law. But what was the best line of attack? First, it had to be non-violent, Gandhi insisted. Second, those in the resistance must be willing to take a beating. They must, as needed, also be willing to go to jail. Were they? In order to ensure that the resistance movement would not falter, Gandhi required congress members to take a vow to follow the dictates of passive resistance. They would place themselves in harm's way, but without striking a blow. The Passive Resistance Association was born specifically to combat TARA.

One of Gandhi's most adamant policies was that no campaigns should be conducted by sleight of hand. There would be no surprise attacks or covert activities. Instead, the *Indian Opinion* gave the world advance notice of every action. If that made sitting ducks of the protesters, then sitting ducks they would be, and proudly. Passive resistance is only effective if the world is watching—and condemning the bullies.

Hundreds of Indian protesters gathered outside the government offices where registrations were being processed. These brave men distributed pamphlets that discussed and condemned the new registration law. Meanwhile, nearby merchants declined to display their vendor's licenses in protest. But most importantly, the Indian community stood fast in their defiance of the new law. By November 30, 1907, the registration deadline, only 511 Transvaal Indians had registered in compliance with the law. The remaining 12,489 Indians had refused.

The British government was quick to act. Non-complying Indians were summoned to court and offered a choice: to leave the Transvaal or be imprisoned. Among them was Gandhi, who was sentenced to two months in prison. He was thrust into a van, driven to a prison, and forced to put on dirty prison garb. Soon, though, he was surrounded by 150 or so other Indians who had also been arrested, many of them for refusing to display vendor's licenses. Gandhi exhorted them to behave courteously and abide by prison rules.

Gandhi continued to exert enormous influence in prison—so much so that a hasty amendment to TARA was drafted and a copy delivered to the prison for his approval and signature. The amended draft allowed Indians the dignity of voluntary registration in lieu of enforced registration, a difference that was meaningful to Gandhi and his followers. Gandhi agreed to the amended registration rules, and he was released from prison. A majority of Indians registered voluntarily before it emerged that General Jan Smuts had issued a false promise. TARA was not withdrawn; it was enacted. Gandhi and the many people now pledged to his cause took the next step: burning their registration cards.

To that end, a crowd of approximately three thousand Indians, of all faiths, gathered around a cauldron set up near a mosque. It was quite the ceremony. Various leaders of the Indian community first gave speeches. A last-minute message was sent out to the government, offering to cancel the card-burning if TARA were repealed. This gesture of peace was greeted by the Transvaal legislature with anger. In a huff, they unanimously passed the bill into law. At about 4 p.m., a volunteer arrived on bicycle bringing the news that the bill had passed. This announcement was greeted by cheers in the crowd.

In his hand, Gandhi had two thousand registration cards, delivered to him freely by their owners. Gandhi then gave a long speech in which he warned the assembled protesters that their actions could result in untold suffering. Nevertheless, any personal harm that should come was preferable to the endurance of the TARA act, he noted. Indians must protect their dignity. He asked if anyone would like to have his card back. No one did. Instead, he was handed several more cards. For the benefit of those who understood only the Gujarati language, Gandhi gave his speech again in that language. Yusuf Mian, a prominent leader in the resistance movement, did the honors. The registration cards were saturated with paraffin oil and set ablaze. As the bonfire rose, fueled by the hated cards, the crowd roared, whistled, and threw their hats in the air. One newspaper article compared the event to the Boston Tea Party.

Gandhi's impassioned words and actions continued to fall on deaf white ears. Fingerprinting and re-registration were the law, now, and laws preventing further Indian immigration had been put into place. Not only did white South African rulers not relent in their discrimination, but also a new insult was born: a new Dutch government ruled that only Christian marriages were legally valid. With this stroke of a pen, thousands of devout Hindu and Muslim wives, who had humbly obeyed the strictures of their religion, were turned into mistresses. Up until this point, the South African revolution led by Gandhi had been almost entirely a male initiative. Men openly refused to follow the laws and were imprisoned. But with the invalidation of their marriages,

Indian women were mobilized. They marched, protested, and were beaten and arrested. Gandhi's wife, Kasturbai, actively joined the protest.

A few weeks later, as Gandhi was traveling for his work, a guard asked him for his registration card. He could produce none, of course, because he had burned it. When he also declined to be fingerprinted, he was arrested and sent before a magistrate in Volksrust for sentencing. He asked the magistrate for the maximum sentence of three months' hard labor. The magistrate, however, was not inclined to cater to Gandhi's martyr wish. He sentenced the activist to two months' hard labor and then gave him the option of paying a twenty-five pound fine instead. Clearly, the magistrate imagined that Gandhi would opt for the fine, but he was mistaken. At the ceremony of burning registration cards, Gandhi had said that he would rather languish in prison than witness a fellow Indian subjected to indignity. He made good on that declaration and went to prison.

The forced labor was grueling. Prisoners were assigned to dig pits, break up rocks, and work in road gangs. He was transferred to a prison in Johannesburg, where he genuinely feared the behavior of some of the prisoners—who were serving time for serious felonies, not for symbolic political infractions. As it turned out, Gandhi's fears were not misplaced. In the communal bathroom, a large man of Kaffir origins told him to get out. When Gandhi told him politely that he would be out momentarily, the other man flew into a rage and jerked him up in the air with the evident intention of flinging him hard on the floor. Gandhi managed to brace himself by clinging to the doorway. He walked away, smiling and peaceful as always, but two of his fellow Indian prisoners burst into tears.

During this stint in prison, Gandhi received the alarming news that his wife, Kasturbai, was seriously ill. She had recently undergone surgery and was hemorrhaging. Gandhi was torn, of course, but he felt that the campaign for Indian rights made a stronger claim on him than did his wife's illness. He wrote her a letter in which he said that he must not pay the fine but, rather, soldier on in prison in defiance of British law, and he hoped she would understand. He said that, even if she were to die while he was in prison, she would always be alive to him and that he would never remarry. He characterized his struggle as not merely political, but religious and therefore "pure."

Gandhi was released from the Volksrust prison in December. But soon he was arrested again and served yet another three-month sentence. Upon his release, he discarded the European clothing that he had, up to that time, affected. A man dressed entirely in traditional Hindu robes and sandals emerged.

In defiance of the new law, Gandhi convinced miners to strike. Long marches were a keystone in Gandhi's strategy of non-violent non-cooperation. Under Gandhi's encouragement, the striking miners dropped their work and marched across South Africa to a new cooperative farm that Gandhi had established, called the Tolstoy Farm. There, the strikers found rudimentary shelter and food so that they did not starve to death as a result of leaving their jobs. This action did, however, end in violence. Many miners were brutally beaten, and some even killed, which badly injured the prestige of the white government in the eyes of the world.

In 1914 the government seemed to relent, finally, and a series of laws were passed that addressed most of the concerns of the South African Indians. Gandhi was finally free to return to India, having achieved a modicum of success. Unfortunately, the hard-won rights of South African Indians were not lasting. In Gandhi's absence, many injustices were reinstated, and discriminations continued against Indians well into the twentieth century. But Gandhi could not know that his South African triumphs were short-lived. He returned to India, feeling that he had accomplished his goals.

Return to India

He went to Chomeran and starts the indige campgain

He settled a dispute

Gandhi returned to India with an international reputation as a successful activist for human and civil rights. He was therefore primed for social action in his home country. A movement to liberate India from British rule was already active, and those most active in that movement naturally hoped Gandhi would lend his reputation and ability to the cause of independence. But Gandhi had other plans.

Despite the abuses of British rule that he had witnessed firsthand in Africa, he was still ambivalent about English rule in India and inclined to accommodation rather than rebellion. He demonstrated his loyalty to the British empire by joining the British military forces that fought in World War I. Many of Gandhi's contemporaries—and even some historians—have criticized him for his participation in war in any form. Given his philosophy of non-violence, they thought military service was, at best, inconsistent. It should be noted, however, that Gandhi limited his military activity to organizing a medical team as he had done in the suppression of the Zulu nation. His was in a "stretcher" brigade, a rudimentary form of ambulance care. In the end, a bout of pleurisy prevented Gandhi even from serving in person.

After the war, Gandhi wished to rediscover the country of his birth. Much had changed, and as was his practice, he wanted to study, observe, and listen before taking action. He traveled for a year to observe the vast country that he had retaken as home. He studied the problems of villagers, listened, and gave speeches. During these treks, he met Rabindranath Tragore, who bestowed on Gandhi the title "mahatma," which means "holy."

Gandhi's first decisive Indian move, in 1915, was to establish another cooperative farm, this one called the Sabarmati ashram. He built this cooperative in Ahmedabad, a town where the principal industry was the manufacture of textiles. And this time, he made the controversial decision to open the community to an untouchable family. Indian untouchables were members of no caste, and as their name implies, Indians born into any of the four castes considered themselves polluted by any significant interaction with the untouchables. Members of this enormous underclass undertook duties that other Indians considered unclean: leather working, cleaning latrines, and scavenging. The inclusion of an untouchable family was the first indication that Gandhi would eventually become the champion of this class of virtually invisible people.

Gandhi's first political move upon return to India was to help the indigo farmers of Champaran. Approached by one of the said farmers, he was at first skeptical. He had to see the conditions for himself. So he traveled to Champaran, a rural province, largely cut off from the rest of the world, even the rest of India. There, wealthy British landowners had been making their fortunes for half a century by forcing their tenants to grow indigo. Indigo was, for a time, a lucrative crop because processing it was the only way to produce the deep blue dye coveted by clothing manufacturers and their consumers. To that end, tenant farmers were required by law to dedicate three out of every twenty arable acres to growing indigo. They then surrendered their indigo crops to their landlords, who accepted them in partial lieu of rent. This system continued with few ripples, enriching the landlords while the Indian farmers did all of the work simply to maintain a living that was barely more than subsistence. The dedication of part of their land to growing indigo meant that these very poor farmers could grow less food, which led to poor nourishment among the workers.

However, prior to Gandhi's arrival in Champaran, things had shifted. New, synthetic dyes had been invented. They were cheaper and easier to manufacture, and the indigo industry was circling the drain. The landlords succeeded for some time in withholding relevant information about the decline of indigo from their tenants. Presenting themselves as magnanimous, they canceled indigo contracts in exchange for exorbitant rent increases of roughly sixty percent. Meanwhile, they also imposed illegal taxes on nearly every institution in which the Champaran farmers might engage. If a couple wanted to get married, they had to pay a tax. Such taxes were also imposed on small and large appliances and most household fixtures. Between the taxes and rent gouging, many Champaran farmers were literally starving. Those who rebelled and threatened not to pay the increased rent were beaten.

Despite the obvious abuses, Gandhi sought to hear the landowners' point of view. He called on representatives to ask for a meeting but was told, in threatening terms, that he had no business in Champaran and that he should go.

Gandhi, of course, had no intention of being bullied into leaving. He dug in and looked for multiple ways to improve the quality of life in Champaran. This led directly to infrastructural improvements. He led the villagers on clean-up projects and got schools and hospitals built. He built another cooperative farm. He also preached his social beliefs, exhorting the local farmers and residents to regard women and untouchables as equals.

Gandhi's meeting with local lawyers proved more successful than his meeting with landowners. Several attorneys were genuinely interested in redressing the plight of the Champaran farmers, but they had made no real headway in the British-controlled judicial system. They were shocked by what Gandhi asked them to be prepared to do: work for free and go to prison. To their credit, after a moment of stunned surprise, the lawyers agreed to Gandhi's tactics.

The people of Champaran had heard of Gandhi, but surprisingly, they did not think of him as a revolutionary or a political activist. The reputation that had preceded Gandhi to Champaran was that of a holy man—and these rural, poorly educated farmers took their holy men seriously. When Gandhi was arrested by the local police, the peasantry swarmed into town and put the fear of chaos into the local authorities. The police had to release their prisoner because he was the only one who could exert any real influence on the crowd.

Reform came swiftly after that, and it is worth noting that no one in the Champaran campaign was beaten and no one arrested other than Gandhi himself. The idea of a massive peasant rebellion was enough to bring the land owners to the table for negotiations. The landlords agreed that a third-party commission should study the case. The commission found in favor of the tenant farmers. In the end, the landowners had to refund 25 percent of what they had extorted from the peasants. Many of them soon sold their land to their tenants. The indigo campaign can therefore be counted among Gandhi's genuine successes.

Overall, 1917 was a successful year for Gandhi. Not only did he bring the Champaran rebellion to a successful conclusion, but he also learned to weave. The classic image of Gandhi— naked to the waist, dressed in little more than a towel, and seated next to a rustic spinning wheel—grew out of Gandhi's belief in a self-sufficient Indian village. In fact, prior to the British invasion, many Indian villages were self-sufficient. They grew their own food, wove their own clothes, educated their own young, and handled their own disputes. Gandhi believed that a return to such independent communities would render the British irrelevant.

However, he hit a snag in the "Buy India" program because the yarn out of which Indian clothes were made were mostly manufactured in British-owned factories. Gandhi then had the good fortune to learn of a group of Baroda Muslims who had offered to weave fabric on rustic instruments if they were supplied with cotton. They had found a set of old, retired spinning wheels and saw the potential to assist the Buy India campaign. Gandhi himself learned to use such a wheel, which led to a redesign of the instrument into a simple, portable wheel that could be easily manufactured in an ashram or village.

Overtaxed

While Gandhi was rescuing the farmers of Champaran, he learned of another hardship that threatened farmers in Kheda. Once his victory in Champaran was secured, he hastened without respite to the next campaign.

In Kheda, Indians owned and farmed their own land, unlike the tenant farmers of Champaran. The Kheda farmers also paid taxes to the British raj. These annual taxes were the sticking point because crops had failed disastrously in Kheda. Farmers had harvested less than 25 percent of their usual annual product, but the British government made no concessions on taxes. The Kheda farmers appealed to the government, and the reply was a discourteous and dismissive "no." As a consequence, farm families in Kheda were on the brink of famine.

Per usual, Gandhi first convinced the local peasants to sign a pledge to the upcoming satyagraha. This pledge was extracted to discourage defection from the cause when circumstances became rough. He then drafted a petition to the government that outlined all the grievances of the locals and declared they would not pay the assigned tax. The British struck back with characteristic brutality, seizing cattle and farms.

Near-famine teetered over into starvation for local subsistence farmers, who had no savings or other assets on which to fall back. Morale slipped, and a few hard-pressed farmers paid their taxes. Gandhi responded by staging a subsidiary protest. A group of protesters overran an onion farm that had been seized by the government, and they harvested all the onions. These looters were arrested, but their action acted as an effective antidote to despair. They were escorted on their way to jail by a crowd of cheering admirers. Though this campaign did not resolve to everyone's satisfaction, it can also be deemed a definite success. The government quickly caved and waived tax payments for the poorest peasants. Only those farmers who could afford to pay were required to do so.

Concession a privilage granted by the Government
teeter: wobble
Subsistence: means of support

Massacre

In 1919 the movement to free India from British rule was growing, but Gandhi had not yet committed himself to its cause. In response to the restlessness and growing dissatisfaction of the Indian masses, the British could have granted concessions—more self-governance, more professional opportunities, and more freedoms. Instead, the British government in India made a move that was reactionary and almost guaranteed to provoke Gandhi into uniting with those who agitated for independence.

The British wrote the Rowlatt Bills, so named for a judge who recommended a crackdown in India when a loosened grip would have been more effective. The Rowlatt Bills introduced serious civil rights violations into India. They deprived Indians, in some circumstances, of the right to a jury trial, allowed for arbitrary imprisonment, and pronounced that even possessing a pamphlet arguing for Indian self rule was an act of treason, punishable by two years in prison. Under the Rowlatt Bills, many political prisoners would not even possess the right to appeal. The Rowlatt Bills were passed and became law, but their provisions were never actually enforced because of the rebellion that followed their passage.

These bills provoked Gandhi's first concerted act of civil disobedience in India. An enormous crowd of Hindus and Muslims, from all walks of life, joined him in an action that looked much like a contemporary "occupy" protest, with the addition of prayer and fasting. Many participants went on strike, closing shops and walking away from their places of employment. Unfortunately, this entirely peaceful, Gandhi-endorsed satyagraha prompted outbreaks of dissatisfaction in other parts of India, and those spontaneous outbursts were not as peaceful.

In Amritsar, a city in the north, four Europeans were killed. British Brigadier General Dyer responded with a display of force that was entirely out of proportion: troops were sent to assault and shoot peaceful protesters. Dyer is also responsible for the reprehensible "crawling order," which legally obliged a number of Indians to crawl on all fours down a street. Some of the soldiers tasked with enforcing the crawling order took it further and ordered Indians to crawl on their stomachs. Anyone who refused was publicly whipped. Dyer quickly followed up on this travesty of human rights by ordering his troops to fire on peacefully-assembled, unarmed protesters.

The events leading up to the Jallianwala Bagh massacre started in April 1919, when the British arrested two popular and high-profile leaders of the independence movement. They were being held in a secret location, so their friends and family did not even know if they were safe. To protest these arrests, a group of Indian nationalists gathered outside the house of the Deputy Commissioner of Amritsar, in the region of Punjab. British soldiers responded by shooting at the crowd, and several peaceful protesters were killed. From that point on, the contingent of Indian nationalists departed from the sacred rules of satyagraha. In the ensuing melee, which lasted for several days in various parts of the Punjab, several Europeans were killed, among them an English missionary who was providing Indian children with a free education. Several government buildings were torched. The British continued to respond with violence and shooting throughout this skirmish.

What ended as a massacre started out as observance of a religious holiday. Thousands of Sikhs, Muslims, and Hindus assembled in a narrow, enclosed public garden known as Jallianwala Bagh to celebrate the Festival of Baisakhi. The purpose of the Baisakhi holy day is to give thanks for harvest. In the combined Indian faiths, it is akin to Thanksgiving. The assembled crowd included pilgrims who had made the trip as a religious rite. Other members of the crowd were peaceful protesters committed to Gandhi's principles of civil disobedience. In general, the crowd was unified by indignation at the arrest of the independence movement leaders who had been detained earlier that month.

Access to and from the garden was limited to narrow, walled streets with small entrances. Effectively, the garden was hemmed in by surrounding houses and other buildings, which formed a barrier around it. General Dyer arrived with troops at about 5:30 in the afternoon. Ninety soldiers entered the gardens, fifty of them armed with Lee-Enfield bolt-action rifles. The armored cars that Dyer had requisitioned for the event were too big to access the narrow pathways into the bagh, so they were used to block the main entrance (also the main exit) of the garden. Without issuing any warning to the crowd, Dyer instructed his troops to block other escape routes.

Again without warning, Dyer ordered his men to fire at will on the densest part of the crowd. The victims were essentially sitting ducks. The soldiers made no attempt to spare women or even children. The shooting continued non-stop for ten minutes and stopped only because the soldiers had run out of bullets. Many people died of gunshot wounds, but others were killed in the stampedes toward the bottlenecked exits. Yet others tried to escape the bullets by jumping into a well, where they drowned. Dyer ordered his men to make no effort to help the wounded.

Various sources disagree about the number of dead and wounded. The British freely admitted that they had used 1,650 bullets, a number they arrived at by counting spent cartridges. They also reported 379 deaths, but that figure has been in dispute ever since. The Indian National Congress estimated that the massacre claimed over 1,500 lives. The British government tried to censor information about the massacre to prevent its news from traveling to England, but the story did get out, and the home British learned of the tragedy several months later.

General Dyer, who had acted largely on his own initiative, was initially complimented on his decisive action. He claimed to be suppressing a "revolutionary army," which totally mischaracterized the unarmed, peaceful protesters. Several months after the massacre, Dyer was subjected to a formal inquiry, in which he adamantly defended his actions. The commissioners appointed to study his actions ultimately condemned them. He served no time in prison, but was removed from his command roughly a year after the massacre.

As more information about the massacre emerged and home British expressed their dismay and horror, opinion about Dyer's actions shifted. British war leader Winston Churchill described the event as "monstrous."

Buy India

Gandhi officially joined the movement for independence following the massacre and the passage of the Rowlatt Bills, and he signified this position by returning his war medals. Under the umbrella of the Indian National Congress, he organized a nationwide campaign of civil disobedience, which called for non-payment of taxes, a boycott of British products, and the closure of many businesses and universities.

Cloth was at the heart of this campaign. Indians had, for many years, been buying British-made fabric and clothes. Even so-called "traditional" Indian garments were likely to be made of this imported material. As a consequence, Indian women no longer spun cloth in their homes, and a cottage industry was all but lost. Gandhi called on his fellow countrymen to desist from purchasing any more British-made fabric and clothing. He called on Indian women to revive the cottage weaving industry, make their own clothes, and sell cloth to the immediate members of their community. Across India, huge bonfires blazed, and English clothing was flung into them by enthusiastic supporters. At this point, Gandhi discarded his long robe and cap, traditional Indian men's attire that he had worn since rejecting Western garb. These items of clothing were flung into a bonfire, and thereafter Gandhi wore his famous one-piece, homespun loin-cloth.

A photo from 1921 shows him at a gathering of men variously clad in European suits or long white robes with long sleeves and turbans. Gandhi's head is shaven, however, and he is naked to the waist. His unselfconscious expression of joy shows how little he cared about being underdressed for the occasion.

In 1922, Gandhi called for the people of the Bardoli district to withhold their taxes. The plan was to start the civil disobedience in Bardoli and then expand to nearby districts, bankrupting the British regional government. However, this carefully-planned campaign never got off the ground because, just prior to its inception, violence and murder broke out in the town of Chauri Chaura. There, protesters aligned with the free India movement set fire to a police station and brutally killed 22 policemen. Gandhi was appalled by the violence, which was in no way the child of his belief in peaceful action and simplicity. He therefore called for a suspension of satyagraha.

Rather than counting their blessings, however, the British again responded with unnecessary force and arrested Gandhi.

During his trial, Gandhi pled guilty, of course, and was sentenced to six years' imprisonment. He served only two of those years because he became terribly ill with appendicitis and had to undergo surgery.

During his years in prison, the independence movement had floundered. Upon his release, Gandhi did not immediately pick up the mantle of leadership in the campaign to free India. He was perturbed by the acrimony that had emerged between Muslims and Hindus, which often flared up into violence. Instead of encouraging reconciliation, the British fanned the flames of religious partisanship by throwing their support behind a Muslim organization that had been created to challenge the Hindu-dominated Indian National Congress. Thus, 1924 found Gandhi performing a 21-day fast to protest the polarization of Muslim and Hindu communities. This humble sacrifice did succeed, briefly, in bringing peace between the two factions.

For a time, Gandhi withdrew from the political sector and focused his efforts on improving the status of the untouchables. By 1925 his efforts made it possible for the untouchables to enter Hindu temples for the first time.

Once again, it took a reactionary move from the British to compel Gandhi back into action. This time, the culprit was Lord Irwin, a British viceroy. Irwin arrogantly proposed to form a commission to recommend changes to the Indian constitution. This commission, as Irwin conceived it, would have no Indian members of any religion, nor would any Indians even be consulted. Irwin's actions galvanized Gandhi. Six years after he had cancelled the plan to withhold taxes in Bardoli, he resurrected the exact same plan and put it into action.

The Bardoli district is a rural region. At that time, it consisted of roughly 137 villages. Physically, the region was around 222 square miles in size, and the population was 88,000. The timing of the Bardoli tax satyagraha could not have been more apt. Floods and famine had decimated the local crops, leaving farmers broke and hungry. However, in the same year, the British announced a tax increase of 22 percent. As a consequence, farm families were faced with the choice of having enough food to eat or paying their taxes. They could not do both.

Under Gandhi's leadership and that of fellow nationalist Sardar Vallabhbhai Patel, the local peasants agreed to withhold their taxes. The government was initially unrelenting, but soon there was not enough tax revenue to run the local government, and it stalled. As the campaign continued, Governor Leslie Wilson appointed a committee to study the issue and make a recommendation. After reviewing the situation in Bardoli, the committee found in favor of the local peasants and upheld their complaint. Tax bills were substantially lowered, and confiscated farms were returned to their original owners. The British government's credibility took another hard hit as a consequence. The media took a strong interest, and even the pro-British *Times of India* covered the campaign extensively. The *Times* characterized Patel as a "Bolshevik" who frequently reported to his puppet-master, Gandhi. One article described the campaign as having "paralyzed" the government. The same article openly recognized the power of the Indian masses to bring about change.

The results of the Bardoli campaign were exactly what Gandhi had hoped for. In fact, they renewed his faith in the patience and discipline of his people and their ability to draw and hold a line in the sand without resorting to violence. No British were attacked, but peacefully protesting Indians were arrested, imprisoned, and beaten. Britain firmly positioned itself as a bully in the eyes of the world. The success of the Bardoli satyagraha loomed large in Gandhi's consciousness. He wrote about it frequently in the ensuing years and generally regarded it as a near-textbook case of a successful satyagraha. With this success in hand, he tweaked his ideas about satyagraha in preparation for the next big campaign. Also encouraged by the traction of the Bardoli protest, the Indian National Congress called for the British to "quit India" within a year.

The Salt March

They marched peacfully through the streets to recrute people and to support making there own salt because the brits made salt and didn't give them much of it

In 1930 a few grains of salt changed the course of India's history. Gandhi had already called on his people to boycott British-made fabric and to withhold taxes imposed by the British. His next move was to challenge the Salt Act of 1882, which gave Brits complete control over the sale of salt. The tax on salt was only a small part of the revenues Britain extracted from India, but having to purchase British-controlled salt was a hardship for India's poor. Salt was not just seasoning, though Gandhi did note that it was the only seasoning routinely used by the poor. At the most basic level, people need some salt to survive. The human body runs, in part, on sodium. In India's hot climate, people sweated out their reserves of salt quickly.

Plans for the salt march were carefully laid. In keeping with Gandhi's insistence that no satyagraha should be covert, newspapers gave notice of the upcoming march and Gandhi's intention to harvest his own salt in defiance of the Salt Act. He also wrote a politely-worded, even warm letter to Lord Irwin, the British Viceroy, addressing him as "Dear friend." In this letter, Gandhi reprehended British policy and also took a moment to condemn Irwin's salary, which he noted was greater than that of Britain's prime minister. More importantly, Irwin's income, Gandhi pointed out, was five thousand times that of the average Indian.

Irwin responded by refusing to meet with Gandhi. Having published advance details of the march, Gandhi was prepared for the possibility of being arrested again, but Irwin considered the salt march laughable and declined to make a preemptive strike. He could not imagine the domino effect it would have because he failed to understand how Gandhi appealed to the ethos and imagination of his fellow countrymen. Irwin mistakenly believed that Gandhi was in failing health and that the salt march was some kind of desperate last hurrah. In a letter to the Secretary of State for India, Irwin declared as fact that Gandhi's blood pressure was high and his heart in poor shape. Irwin went so far as to predict that Gandhi would die within a year. Clearly, Irwin had not taken the measure of Gandhi's wiry frame, boundless energy, and vegetarian diet.

Gandhi kicked off the salt boycott with his famous march to the sea at Dandi. He started out from his ashram on March 12, 1930. Huge crowds had spent the night nearby so as to be ready to accompany him in the morning. He left his farm in Ahmedabad and walked, on foot, to the Arabian Sea. Though he was sixty-one at the time and had survived multiple serious illnesses, Gandhi was spry. He walked at such a brisk pace that his younger followers, who numbered in the thousands, often had trouble keeping up with him. Some of his companions suffered fatigue and minor foot injuries and had to resort to a bullock-drawn cart. Gandhi's fellow travelers had also take the precaution of discretely bringing a horse, in case the Mahatma tired and needed to ride, yet he never mounted it. Gandhi's only assistance on the march was a bamboo walking stick with an iron tip. He said that marching twelve miles a day in two installments with a midday break was "child's play."

They passed through 48 villages, always taking the time to address local villagers and recruit them for the cause of independence. Many villagers made donations to their cause, and more remarkably, a number of British officials took the opportunity to hand in their resignations.

Gandhi set off from his ashram accompanied by 79 handpicked nationalists. He made sure that the group represented the diversity of India. One marcher was Muslim, one Christian; two were untouchables. The remainder were caste Hindus. The march steadily gained more followers as it proceeded until the parade of people was two miles long and several thousand strong. Gandhi excluded women from his starting companions because, he said, to include women would put the British opponent at an unfair disadvantage. The British would see the women and refrain from attack. However, as the march progressed across India, women joined the throng of other followers.

The marchers arose and got back on the road every morning at 6:30. Gandhi, ever energetic and multi-tasking, gave interviews to the media at various stops, and he even found time to do some more of his own writing. He also wove every day. There were mornings when he was already up by 4 a.m., scribbling by the light of an oil lamp because the sun was not yet up. Meanwhile, in the villages he visited, he asked for nothing but the simplest food and water. He commanded his followers in no uncertain terms to ask for nothing that would represent a hardship for the village. The followers slept out in the open and sang as they marched to keep their spirits high.

As Gandhi marched through the villages of India, admirers strew his path with green leaves. Other Indians fasted and prayed. The journey took a little over three weeks, and it took 24 days to cover the 240-mile distance. The route took the marchers through villages in Bardoli from whence Gandhi had also handpicked some of his fellow marchers. All of his followers wore simple white robes, called "khadi." This stream of white-robed pilgrims prompted someone to nickname the march the "white flowing river."

Once he arrived in Dandi, he broke only one law: once, at the sea, he picked up a salt rock, and as he did, one of his companions shouted, "Hail, deliverer!" After taking possession of a token amount of salt in defiance of the Salt Act, Gandhi gave a very brief speech calling on all Indians to resist British occupation at a number of levels. He told them to make their own salt, burn English clothes, spin their own cloth, avoid drinking alcohol, set aside the practice of untouchability, and treat men of all faiths as brothers. The crowd of followers surrounding him followed suit, reached down to the sand, and gathered symbolic quantities of salt.

In the weeks that followed, satyagraha spread like an epidemic. Indians all over the country took Gandhi's advice. More bonfires were lit to burn English clothing, and liquor stores were picketed. Most of all, Indians learned how to make their own salt. The Indian National Congress had published how-to pamphlets on salt manufacture for personal use. Bombay police found an illegal salt-making enterprise on the very roof of the Indian National Congress. A photograph from this period pictures a protester holding up a sign that urged Indians not to travel abroad but, rather, to enrich India by staying at home. Tens of thousands of nationalists were imprisoned, among them the future Indian prime minister Jawaharlal Nehru. Several protesters were killed.

Following the salt march, police delayed in arresting Gandhi, giving him time to prepare a carefully worded letter to his followers. In part, the letter exhorted all Indians to keep their resistance non-violent, and it promised, in no uncertain terms, that full independence could be won with satyagraha. Furthermore, the letter indicated, India had an opportunity to set an example of peaceful revolution for the rest of the world.

The police caught up with Gandhi about three miles outside Dandi. The Mahatma was sleeping, and they rudely woke him by shining a flashlight in his face. When the charges were read at Gandhi's insistence, he learned that he was being arrested under an 1827 law, dating back to before the raj, which said that the government could arrest someone without trial or assigning a fixed sentence.

In Gujarat, as part of a carefully organized protest, 2,500 members of the Indian National Congress attempted to invade the Dharasana Saltworks, which lay 150 miles north of Bombay. Their objective was to enter the factory peacefully and take the salt, which was, according to Gandhi, the Indian's birthright. As it transpired, none of the brigade got near the salt.

Because Gandhi had been arrested, it fell on the poet Sarojini Naidu to lead this satyagraha. Before they began their deliberate trespass, she reminded the volunteers not to raise an arm in their own defense, even to shield themselves from harm. Gandhi's and Kasturbai's second son, Manilal Gandhi, was in the first group of men who approached the salt pans, making their way around ditches to an armed guard and a barbed wire stockade. The police who surrounded the salt works warned them to stop, but they kept slowly walking forward. The police wielded deadly lathis—steel-covered sticks—with which they proceeded to beat the protesters. As instructed, the nationalists did nothing to defend themselves or fight back. A newspaper article reporting on the event describes the sound of the clubs coming down on "unprotected skulls" as a "sickening whack."

After the first group of volunteers had been laid low, the next contingent approached and the scenario was repeated. Those who wanted to help the wounded soon ran out of stretchers and had to improvise carriers out of blankets. These were soon soaked in blood.

Despite the brutal treatment of the forerunners, the volunteers continued their march undaunted. The trespass and beatings went on for hours, but the nationalists changed tactics at one point. Instead of continuing forward, they entered the Saltworks yard and sat down. The police responded with the same brutality. They starting dragging the trespassers along the ground and throwing them into ditches.

By 11 a.m., the temperature outside was 116 degrees in the shade. The only news reporter on the scene at that point was Webb Miller, but his story was picked up by dozens of newspapers, and the news of the Saltworks satyagraha was heard around the world. Webb made his way to the nearby hospital and counted 320 wounded nationalists. Two of the volunteers had died.

A letter from the British viceroy in India to King George V provides some insight into the wholehearted contempt that the British felt for the Indians while also demonstrating the British inability to gauge the importance of the salt satyagraha. The letter minimized the brutality of the police attack on the nationalists, describing their injuries as "minor" and accusing the volunteers of exaggerating their pain. The letter went on to accuse many volunteers of "playing dead" by lying on the ground as if they were unconscious, and it summed up the action as "propaganda."

Once again, Britain had acted the part of the bully, assaulting an unarmed and peaceful opponent. The media reportage helped Gandhi to hold up a mirror in which the British officials in India could see themselves as the Indians and, increasingly, the rest of the world saw them. It became impossible for some of these officials to maintain the illusion that they were benevolent importers of civilization. Many officials resigned. From this point, local and regional police frequently refused to break up or stifle demonstrations.

The Untouchables

He fasted to help untouchables
lives ~~~~~ and helped to up
Wimens Statas in society
He went to indon but was soon
arrested

The path to Indian independence was a long game with many starts and stops. It had taken Gandhi nearly twenty years to bring about limited reforms in South Africa. It took another twenty years to free India. Though his fans often questioned his delays and tactics, it is clear from both his letters and his actions that he never lost sight of the end goal, and the historical perspective reveals that he had an unerring sense of timing. Satyagraha was clearly harder and more time-consuming than an armed resistance, but it was the more honorable path. Through civil disobedience, India could free itself from tyranny while preserving a commitment to the peaceful ethics of all its major religions.

Despite the fact that Gandhi was in prison, the British found it virtually impossible to retake the reins in India following the salt march. Nationalists had seized control of Bombay. Early in 1931, Gandhi and other leaders were released from prison, and Gandhi negotiated the Gandhi-Irwin pact. Signed by Lord Irwin, then the British viceroy in India, and Gandhi, it stipulated that Indians would be allowed to manufacture their own salt. It also provided for the release of all those Indians imprisoned during the salt satyagraha. For Gandhi's part, he agreed to put a stop to the salt satyagraha. Many Indians were dissatisfied with this intermediate measure and its meager concessions. In particular, the Gandhi-Irwin pact made no provision for future independence from British occupation. Gandhi himself may have put his faith in Irwin's invitation to participate in roundtable talks in London.

Gandhi traveled to London with high hopes. Unfortunately, these talks turned out to be not much more than a time-wasting formality. From the start of the talks, it was obvious that the British had never even considered relinquishing control of India. The talks were also badly marred by obvious polarization and bickering among the various Indian participants. As a consequence, the Indian message was blurred and ineffective.

Gandhi's chief success was his ability to teach by example. Throughout his stay in London, he maintained the gentle demeanor, simple clothing, and humble lifestyle that had made him so admired in India. The Gandhi who presented himself for negotiations in London had traveled, spiritually and philosophically, a long way from the young man who bought first-class train tickets and wore European suits when he went to South Africa. In London, Gandhi lodged in the East End among the city's working poor. The English found it impossible not to love him. Even the textile workers in

Lancashire greeted him enthusiastically—despite the fact that Gandhi's boycott on British fabrics had been a hardship for them.

The London talks and Gandhi's subsequent travel in France, Switzerland, and Italy kept him away from India for most of a year. He then had little time to enjoy his return because he was arrested almost immediately and put back in prison by India's Lord Willingdon, India's new British viceroy.

The failure of the London talks even to consider the possibility of India's liberation renewed Gandhi's commitment to independence. But he was also deeply disturbed by the continued plight of the untouchables. Gandhi popularized the term 'Harijan,' which means "children of God," to refer to the untouchable class. He took the term from the medieval female poet Gangasati, who used the term to refer to herself as an outcast. Up to that point in time, untouchables had been referred to dismissively as "dalit."

While in prison, he undertook a fast-to-the-death in protest of abuses against the untouchable class. He was moved to this drastic measure by a proposed new law that would put the Harijan in a separate electorate. If made law, Gandhi believed, this proposal would perpetuate the abuse and discrimination to which the untouchables were already subjected.

Gandhi was already rake-thin when he began his fast, and he soon became dangerously ill. Both India and Britain reacted quickly. Many temples opened their doors to the Harijan. Britain announced that it would alter its plans for a separate untouchable electorate. The Brits also drafted a Poona Pact, which provided reserved seats for the Harijan within the Provincial and Central Legislatures. Harijan leader Bhimrao Ramji Ambedkar traveled to Yerwada Central Jail in Pune to co-sign the agreement with Gandhi.

Gandhi stayed busy in prison. From his cell, he launched a new publication, the *Harijan*, to call attention to the human and civil rights violations to which the untouchables were subjected. Soon the journal was appearing in English, Gujarati, and Hindi. Some claim that, of all Gandhi's publications, the *Harijan* was the most influential in the campaign for India's independence. Though it was unaffiliated with any party, the *Harijan* was a mouthpiece for Gandhi's non-stop meditation on morality. As such, the journal did not confine its information to the problem of the untouchables but instead covered a wide array of topics of general interest to India. A

1935 issue of the journal, for instance, featured an article, authored by Gandhi, about the merits of soybeans.

Upon his release from prison, Gandhi continued campaigning for the untouchables. He undertook a pilgrimage of twelve thousand miles. He was surprised by the violent pushback that he encountered among his fellow Hindus who did not agree that the Harijan should be uplifted. In some towns and villages, he was denied access to the temple, and there were three attempts on his life by Hindu extremists. But Gandhi did not waver in his determination to improve the untouchables' lot. In 1933 he donated the Sabarmati ashram to the untouchables, and he vowed that he would not return there until India had achieved independence.

He himself relocated to the village of Shegaon in central India, where he started up the Sevagram ashram. The English translation of 'Sevagram' is "village of service." And that is what Gandhi proposed to make the new ashram: an experiment in village sustainability. In addition to farming and teaching the young, the village also engaged in naturopathic healing. Gandhi placed great emphasis on hygiene, especially keeping the latrines from becoming septic. At Sevagram, Gandhi continued his campaign to liberate untouchables.

Several people from that community were hired to work in the kitchen.

Gandhi was also concerned about the inferior status of women in India. To that end, he encouraged cottage crafts and industries, such as cloth-making and weaving, that allowed women to earn their own money. He opposed a number of practices that were endorsed by Hindu texts and practices. The position of women within the Hindu community was indeed dire. Female infanticide was not unknown since girl babies were considered a drain on a family's resources. Girls were also likely to be illiterate. Investing in their education was often considered a waste of time and money. If a girl became a widow, Hindu belief discouraged her from ever remarrying.

Gandhi opposed all of these practices. He also opposed veil-wearing, or *purdah*, and dowries. Dowries, he believed, reduced women to tradable commodities. Though he himself was a participant in a child marriage, he opposed child marriages. Moreover, though he was the product of a polygamous union, he opposed polygamy through word and example. While the laws of India and his religion permitted him multiple wives, he remained monogamous and faithful to his child bride, Kasturbai. In fighting for better women's rights, Gandhi received invaluable help from Madeleine Slade, a British woman who learned of Gandhi's teachings and traveled to India to join him at the Sevagram ashram.

World War II

He fought and protested
to get indeas independence
but they didn't find a meeting
point easily and there was
chaos in india that wouldn't stop
and another assasination failed

With characteristic insensitivity, the British dragged India into World War II without actually asking the Indians. Gandhi and the Indian National Congress agreed that they would offer no support to the war effort without a promise of future independence. When the British continued to withhold this promise, the congress asked Gandhi to reboot the non-violent fight against British occupation. Gandhi was torn. One of the principles of non-violent non-cooperation, as he had forged it, was not to take advantage of any external hardship that divided the opponent. He had acted on this principle in the past, ending campaigns because the British had other conflicts to settle.

Clearly a world war put the British at a disadvantage and divided their resources, so Gandhi launched a campaign that was limited to freedom of expression. The British had redoubled their restrictions on "sedition," by which they meant any public criticism of the British and their regime. Criticism of the war became illegal under this new crackdown, which created an almost perfect stage for a new satyagraha.

Gandhi referred to it as an "individual satyagraha" even though it resulted in the arrest of 23,000 people. The individual satyagraha simply asked an individual to find a public place and start spouting anti-war rhetoric until the police came to arrest him. Gandhi handpicked the first volunteers for this project, and Vinoba Bhave received the honor of launching the campaign. He made his way to Paunar in mid-October, 1940, where he issued a criticism of the war on purely pacifist grounds. He was duly arrested, as were Jawaharlal Nehru and Brahmadatta Nirmal in quick succession, followed by other members of the Indian National Congress. Such was Gandhi's influence at this point in his career that volunteers jockeyed for the chance to be arrested and thrown in prison. Shortly after the first three freedom-of-speech arrests, a contingent of governmental officials asked to participate. Gandhi tried to talk them out of it. Would they not be more effective if they remained in their positions of leadership, he wondered. In the end, however, they convinced him and were arrested.

The ongoing British presence in India in the 1940s contributed to factionalism among Indian nationals. The British failure to move toward leaving India also provoked a break with Gandhi's successful regime of non-violence. A new leader, Subhas Chandra Bose, emerged, and he advocated overthrowing Britain by force. Bose ran Free India Radio from Berlin, Germany, and he solicited help from both the German

Nazi party and the Japanese in ridding India of the Brits. Though Bose's efforts to liberate India were entirely unsuccessful, he did provoke divisions among Indian nationalists that persisted after independence.

When Japan entered the war, Britain became more desperate to accommodate the Indian nationalist movement in order to secure India's cooperation for the Allied forces. British Prime Minister Winston Churchill sent an emissary to India to negotiate reforms. Superficially, the reforms offered some progress, but Gandhi rejected them outright because the proposals made room for princely provinces to secede from a federated India. Gandhi could foresee that such a loophole would result in India's partition.

When Britain failed to design a plan for India's independence, the Indian National Congress officially called for Britain to "quit India." To launch this movement, Gandhi gave a speech that called for a recommitment to non-violent, selfless action. Only through non-violence could India achieve the future that it sought, he said. Independence gained through violence could well end in a dictatorship. In the same speech, he exhorted Indians not to hate the British people and not to act out of hate. He also warned that collaboration with Japan would likely mean exchanging one master for another.

The British did not even wait 24 hours before throwing Gandhi into prison again, along with most of the leaders of the Indian National Congress. This time, the rebels were held at Aga Khan Palace in Poona. Kasturbai followed her husband to prison voluntarily, though the prospect terrified her. Britain blamed the spontaneous outbursts of violence that followed Gandhi's arrest on Gandhi himself. Responding to the flare-up of violent incidents, Churchill issued his own speech. In it, he declared that, as the king's first minister, he would not "preside over the liquidation of the empire."

Meanwhile, India continued its downward spiral toward division and dissent amongst religious sects. A leading voice for Muslim separation was Muhammad Ali Jinnah. Jinnah was the leader of the Muslim League, which had set itself in opposition to the Hindu-majority Indian National Congress.

Ghandi suffered a great loss while incarcerated in Poona: Kasturbai, his wife of 61 years, died in his arms. When he contracted a dangerous case of malaria, he was released from prison. He went to Juhu Beach, where a friend loaned him the use of a seaside cottage for his recovery. There he prayed, took long beach walks, met with friends, and processed his grief over Kasturbai's death.

Late in 1944, Gandhi agreed to take a meeting with Muslim League leader Jinnah in the latter's home in Bombay. Since 1940, Jinnah had been agitating for Muslims to have their own state, and he had gained a lot of traction for his cause. While members and leaders of the Indian National Congress were protesting the war and being imprisoned, Jinnah's group, the Muslim League, provided valued assistance to the Allies. Gandhi, however, had always favored a united India. Throughout his lifetime, he had looked for bridges between his own Hindu faith and other belief systems. He had worked happily and effectively with Muslims, Parsee, Jains, Christians, and others on common causes. He sincerely believed that the Indian National Congress represented the interests of all Indians, as did most of its leaders.

Gandhi and Jinnah met and talked over a period of two weeks, but they were able to find no common ground. Gandhi, the master broker of compromise, failed to find a win–win solution to their disparate goals. Gandhi agreed that India should discuss the possibility of a Muslim state once India was free of the British, but Jinnah was steadfastly unwilling to wait for independence. He wanted a partitioned Muslim state immediately. Jinnah's efforts would soon result in the creation of Pakistan.

After the defeat of Germany, Britain elected a Labour government that was friendly to the idea of an independent India. At long last, in 1945, Britain announced plans for quitting the country in which they had been so unwelcome for so many years. The Simla Conference was set up to manage the transition. Gandhi attended the conference as a private individual, declining a leadership role because he did not want to run afoul of Jinnah. His silence did not make the conference a success, however. The conference at Simla floundered and failed to achieve any real end because the All-India Muslim League would not cooperate with the Indian National Congress. The Muslim League representatives continued to make an independent Muslim state their only talking point, which caused a breakdown in negotiations.

The British remained committed to Indian independence, however, and sent a delegation to Delhi to navigate the transfer of powers. The British attitude toward India had definitely changed, and the components of independence swiftly fell into place. Jawaharlal Nehru, who had participated in civil disobedience with Gandhi and had been imprisoned with him, was elected prime minister of the newly independent state. Nehru had spent nine of the previous twenty-five years in prison, outstripping even Gandhi, who had spent only six years behind bars. With Gandhi's blessing, Nehru replaced Gandhi as the face of independence and Indian leadership. This was despite the fact that Nehru did not always agree with Gandhi's principles. For instance, Nehru put much less faith in traditional village crafts than did Gandhi, and Nehru embraced a degree of Western modernity that Gandhi rejected.

The Indian National Congress somewhat reluctantly accepted a British-designed constitution. The new instrument gave considerable autonomy to individual provinces, which made both Nehru and Gandhi uncomfortable. Despite this attempt to accommodate religious and regional differences, Jinnah rejected the proposal and called for a Muslim day of action. This message was widely interpreted as a call for violence. Over five thousand Indians, most of them Hindu, were killed in the ensuing riots around Calcutta. Fear and resentment spread to other parts of the country, and the violence continued. The masses quickly forgot the commitment to peace and simplicity that Gandhi had so patiently and carefully preached.

Gandhi, now an old man, swung into action. He undertook another walking pilgrimage, frequently propped up by supporters under each arm. He walked hundreds of miles, visiting village after village and pleading with the residents to desist from force. In Bihar, he threatened to start another fast. Two more assassination attempts were made on him during this time. Some people listened, and some regions laid down arms, but civil conflict in India had found a life of its own, and neither Gandhi nor Jinnah seemed able to stop it.

In 1947, Jinnah and Gandhi got together to issue a joint plea to stop the violence in India, but it fell on mostly deaf ears. Despite the spiraling chaos, Britain continued apace with its plans to liberate India. Lord Mountbatten arrived in India early that year with plans to make India self-governed in around six months. Mountbatten's plan provided for a separate Muslim state, which became modern-day Pakistan. Mountbatten believed partition was an inevitability and the only way to reconcile the demands of the Muslim League with the Indian National Congress. Jinnah and Nehru agreed to the new terms, and Gandhi regretfully joined them in endorsing the creation of Pakistan.

Independence

endorsed: to aprove ~~~~

Partition: to divide

they became an independent
state but gahndi didn't think
it was a success chaos went
throughout india

India officially became independent at midnight of August 14, 1947. Enormous celebrations marked the event. Gandhi was not among the happy partiers, however. In brief, after fighting for Indian independence for almost thirty years, he felt strongly that he had failed. Peace had not been kept. India was harshly divided along religious lines, and now Britain, as a lasting legacy, had endorsed those religious conflicts by carving India into two separate states.

History has proven that Gandhi's fears were justified. Partition did not curb the violence in India; instead, it accelerated it. To the careless British politician, it must have seemed that a region with a majority of Muslims would be content to be a separate Muslim state. What the British and many Indian nationalists failed to understand was that partition would make despised minorities of the many residents in Pakistan who were not Muslim and the many residents of India who were not Hindu. In the newly-formed state of Pakistan, nineteen million Hindus and one and a half million Sikhs were disenfranchised. In India, 38 million Muslims were similarly reduced to unwelcome minority status. Millions of people left their homes and tried to cross the border to the country that had been assigned to their faith.

Chaos, hatred, and violence ensued. In and around Calcutta, in particular, assaults, beatings, and murder were common occurrences. Gandhi started another to-the-death fast, determined not to eat until local leaders committed themselves to peace. This drastic action did achieve a ceasefire in Calcutta, but elsewhere in India and Pakistan, violence continued. Gandhi traveled to Delhi, which was plagued by some of the worst destruction. When he got there and witnessed firsthand the religious extremism and violence that had taken hold, he started another fast in Birla House, a lovely mansion overlooking formal gardens. It would be the final stop on his life's journey.

Gandhi was almost eighty years old, and no one predicted that he would survive a long fast. His kidneys failed two days in. In response, over a hundred community leaders wrote and signed a peace accord. Gandhi ended his fast, but the peace was neither real nor lasting, as a bomb detonated at a prayer meeting in Birla House quickly showed.

Murder

The exploding bomb—which miraculously left no one injured—was part of an assassination attempt that was planned over several months by a group of Hindu extremists. Gandhi survived the bomb and another attempt on his life by the same group, but his days were numbered by the time he moved into Birla House. The assassination was carefully plotted by Nathuram Godse, Narayan Apte, and Vishnu Ramakrishna Karkare. They cased Birla House and purchased weapons for the purpose. As part of their scheme, they studied Gandhi's schedule. It quickly became clear that he had an established routine, which involved holding prayer daily in the Birla House gardens.

The conspirators' reasons for wanting Gandhi dead were mixed, self-contradictory, and irrational in the way that psychotic reasoning usually is. In a nutshell, they blamed Gandhi for the mistreatment of Hindus in Pakistan. At his murder trial, Godse specifically accused Gandhi of accommodating Muslims at the expense of Hindus. In general, the conspirators believed that Gandhi's policy of non-violence had created hardships for the brethren of their faith.

Late in the afternoon on January 30, 1948, all three conspirators hired tongas and rode to Birla House. There were about five hundred people on the prayer ground, and Godse mixed in with them. Apte and Karkare found their way to him and flanked him, one on each side. The crowd parted, and Gandhi made his way across, propped up by his great nieces. Gandhi greeted his many friends and followers as Godse reached for the Beretta in his pocket, slid the catch off, and then darted forward.

Godse shot Gandhi three times with a Beretta nine millimeter pistol. Despite multiple prior attempts on his life, Gandhi had never employed bodyguards or even seriously vetted people who got close to him, so it was relatively easy for his assassin to get within point-blank range. Gandhi's last words were "Oh, God." Godse made no effort to get away but, rather, stood in place with a smoking gun in his hand. Eventually, a Royal Indian Air Force man in uniform jumped at the murderer, beat him on the face, and forced the gun out of his hand. The assembled crowd went crazy, crying "Kill him, kill him!" as the police led Godse away. Apte and Karkare blended in with the crowd and got away. Gandhi died two hours later.

The co-conspirators took a train to Bombay and were apprehended and arrested several days later, along with several others who had supported the crime. They were duly tried in the Punjab High Court at Peterhoff. Godse and Apte were sentenced to death by hanging. Karkare was sentenced to life imprisonment. Other conspirators who had participated in the planning and arming of the crime were also tried and sentenced.

Gandhi's funeral took place the day immediately following his murder. Thousands of mourners choked the city streets as his funeral procession made its way to the pyre where he was cremated.

Conclusion

It has become a cliché to say that one person can make a difference, but the life of Mahatma Gandhi confronts us with the enduring truth of that statement. He was not born to any particular greatness. He showed little, if any, real talent growing up. He was a middling student. There is no indication that any of his teachers felt they were in the presence of greatness.

The government sinecure that he was in line to inherit was certainly an unearned privilege—before it vanished. It's safe to say that, as a young lawyer struggling to find work in

Bombay, he did not strike his acquaintances as a man with an iron destiny. And yet, whilst failing as a Bombay lawyer, he did reveal a glimmer of the man he would become. He refused to make money by betraying his principles and hiring ambulance chasers. Faced with unemployment and poverty, he would not do the wrong thing.

In South Africa, we begin to see his ability to broker a peace between two bitterly feuding parties. His boss Abdullah and his adversary Tyeb Sheth were locked in a hateful conflict that threatened both their reputations, yet out of this impossible impasse, Gandhi was able to bring about a peace. In its way, the conclusion to the Abdullah–Sheth crisis was a microcosm of the peace Gandhi brokered between the British and India.

He had a masterful ability to pinpoint a symbol that could galvanize the masses. A bonfire of registration cards, a shard of salt from the Arabian Sea, an antique spinning wheel— these carefully chosen images burned their way into the imaginations of Indians across the world and also made their way into the consciences of Europeans and Americans. In the last third of his life, Gandhi turned himself into a symbol of Hindu simplicity with his simple, homespun loin-cloth and his fingers rapidly plying the product of his spinning wheel.

It's impossible to say exactly what moved people to revere and follow him, let alone be imprisoned and beaten by the thousands on his behalf. No doubt, his ever-gentle demeanor had a hand in that. His perpetual grace and joy, even in the face of terrible hardship, must have won some hearts and minds. His genuine ability to treat all men and women as brothers and sisters—whether Hindu, Muslim, Parsee, Sikh, Christian, Harijan, and Zulu— must have won even more.

Gandhi is rightfully remembered as the father of practical civil disobedience. But the drama of his passive resistance campaigns threatens to obliterate the other Gandhi—who believed that his first mission was always to help the poorest members of his community. Many Gandhi biographies minimize his efforts on behalf of the untouchables. But Gandhi saw untouchability as the single most important social issue facing an independent India. Untouchability was a disfiguring scar on the face of Hinduism, he believed. This Gandhi, the one biographers sometimes forget, would rather have walked forty miles to feed a starving family than lobby for political change.

Perhaps Gandhi's greatest achievement, overall, was the way the way he walked his talk. He asked others to go to prison for their beliefs, but he himself served many prison terms. He asked others to take a beating for their beliefs, so he took a terrible beating and put himself repeatedly in the line of fire. He asked others to revive village crafts, and he himself was rarely seen far from a spinning wheel. He asked others to obey Hindu commandments, for he himself ate no meat and remained faithful to one woman his entire life. For these reasons and others, his name has become a synonym for peace, change, and enlightenment. It is safe to say that no one aspires to leadership without studying his life story.

After his death, a political cartoon surfaced that shows Gandhi in conversation with Martin Luther King, Jr. In the cartoon, Gandhi says this:

"The odd thing about assassins, Dr. King, is that they think they've killed you."

Please enjoy the first two chapters of Saint Padre Pio: In the Footsteps of Saint Francis, written by Michael J. Ruszala, as available from Wyatt North Publishing.

Saint Padre Pio: In the Footsteps of Saint Francis

Introduction

In an age that smirks at the mention of miracles, sin, angels, and demons, St. Pio of Pietrelchina has emerged as a figure of immense popularity, attracting fascination, veneration, and also emulation. Padre Pio, who once wrote in a letter, "I am a mystery to myself," is certainly a mystery to all who know of him. To those who moved beyond mere credulity, he became an inspiration to embrace the fullness of faith. Perhaps that is why his shrine in outlying San Giovanni Rotondo, Italy, is second only to the Vatican itself in annual number of pilgrims and why Italian Catholics now report to praying more for St. Pio's intercession than for that of any other saint.

This book is a concise introduction to Padre Pio's life, especially as compared to the example and journey of his spiritual father, St. Francis of Assisi. If St. Francis is said to be the most popular saint of all time, Franciscan Capuchin Padre Pio is perhaps the most popular saint of *our* times. It is no wonder: Padre Pio miraculously bore the wounds of Jesus in his living body, prophesied the future, read the secrets of hearts, and traveled across the world in a split second. He was also a man of holy boldness, unafraid to offend in charity for the sake of truth or to call out sin for what it was. And he was a favorite of Pope St. John Paul II, who canonized him in 2002.

Given that he passed only in 1968, it is remarkable to think that such a spiritual "superhero" could exist in our modern age. How could he even survive in it? In truth, he barely did—even in the Church. We can marvel at the depth of his involvement in the spiritual world and be reminded of it in the face of our culture of skepticism, but if we can find anything truly in common with this saint, perhaps it is the hardship and crushing misfortune that he faced in this world. He was a man of sorrows who knew how to accept God's will prayerfully even when it hurt and who, despite everything, had the courage to uplift others cheerfully by saying, "Pray, hope, and don't worry."

Through not spared from misfortune, he was spared those things that cloud us from perceiving the world in a truly spiritual way. Perhaps that is why Padre Pio offers us just the message we need to hear.

Chapter 1

St. Padre Pio was truly a man in the world but not of the world. It was as if St. Francis himself, called by some the most Christ-like man who ever lived, had re-emerged in our own times. Like St. Francis, the father of his order and patron saint, Padre Pio bore the stigmata—the miraculous imprint of the five wounds of Christ—in his body. Both were singularly driven by love of Christ and gave complete abandon to him. On that account, St. Francis and Padre Pio were each sharply countercultural in living a life of extreme austerity and piety. Both embraced redemptive suffering in the midst of devastating illnesses and spite from those around them. Both utterly shunned the world and its glory while being hailed as living saints by the masses during their own lifetimes. Both were surrounded by diverse, inexplicable and miraculous phenomena and had great efficacy in their prayers. Both waged dramatic battles with the spiritual forces of evil. Both had great zeal for the Eucharist and devotion to the Blessed Virgin Mary. And both were canonized as saints by the Church in a remarkably short period of time after their deaths, becoming the subject of much devotion among the faithful.

Padre Pio was guided throughout his life by the spirituality and example of St. Francis. His parents, Grazio Mario Forgione and Maria Giuseppa di Nunzio, were faithful Catholic peasants and had particular devotion to the Saint of Assisi as protector of the poor. The future Padre Pio (or Father Pio), born as Francesco

Forgione in 1887, followed his baptismal namesake from a young age, even dedicating himself to St. Francis at the tender age of five. Young Francesco Forgione, who experienced a number of visions of St. Francis throughout his life, was impressed by the admirable, cheerful demeanor of a Capuchin Franciscan by the name of Fra Camillo, who often visited Francesco's hometown of Pietrelcina in southern Italy. Francesco later entered the novitiate in 1903 at Fra Camillo's monastery at Morcone, about 10 miles away, and pursued Christian perfection under the Rule of St. Francis for the rest of his life.

Though not born a saint, Padre Pio was very much morally and spiritually awake from a young age. Ordained a priest in 1910, the Capuchin friar was known for being stern and forthright in shaking the self-complacent, but when the situation warranted, he could be gentle and even playful. He rarely left his monastery, and his care for souls was primarily spiritual—interceding for his spiritual children, hearing confessions, and providing guidance for long hours each day. While always living in the midst of strong Christian communities, he lived at a time when society in general was more skeptical and when the then-unified national government of Italy was hostile to the Catholic faith. Padre Pio lived until the age of 81, suffering together with the Savior, and was canonized by Pope St. John Paul II in 2002.

Despite and, indeed, because of his prayer and solitude, he could not help but catch the modern world off guard by reports of his miraculous stigmata, his numerous healings, and his knowledge of events and secret thoughts that it was impossible for him to know humanly.

This account of the life and ministry of Padre Pio considers in a special way how he lived out his vocation as a Franciscan and how he brought the spirituality of St. Francis to flesh in his times. We will follow him from his early life in Pietrelchina to his formation with the Capuchin friars and his ultimate assignment to the monastery at San Giovanni Rotondo. We will see how, like St. Francis, Padre Pio offered himself as a victim to God through his many trials in life. We will also look at the many gifts that God gave him and how they built up the faith of those around him.

Understanding the Franciscan dimension of Padre Pio is important for understanding his message and spirituality since it was so important to him personally. May this immersion in the lives of St. Francis and Padre Pio challenge us beyond our comfort zone and impel us to give ourselves to Christ more completely. As St. Francis exhorted his brothers in his last days, "Let us begin to serve the Lord our God, for up until now we have made but little progress" (St. Bonaventure, *Life of St. Francis,* 4.1).

Made in the USA
San Bernardino, CA
21 February 2017